Forgiveness

Forgiveness

by
Malcolm Smith

P. O. Box 471692
Tulsa, Oklahoma 74147-1692

Forgiveness
ISBN 1-880089-13-0
Copyright © 1992 by Malcolm Smith
Malcolm Smith Ministries
P. O. Box 29747
San Antonio, Texas 78229

Published by:
Pillar Books & Publishing Co.
P. O. Box 471692
Tulsa, Oklahoma 74147-1692
United States of America

Cover design: DB & Associates

Book production: sigma graphics, ltd.

Editor: Elizabeth Sherman

TABLE OF CONTENTS

Chapter Four

UNLIMITED POWER THROUGH
RELEASING THE DEBT

Forgiveness

Chapter One

HOLY RENOVATION

Have you found yourself avoiding the subject of forgiveness? Do you feel justified in your anger or your acts of retaliation? Then it is likely you are a believer who is living far below the life Jesus came to give you.

I find that many thousands of believers in today's world have a faith that lacks the present tense. They live almost exclusively looking toward a great tomorrow in heaven with little or no thought about how to live in the here and now today. A great many of them feel that, having invited Christ into their hearts, there is nothing more to do but to become involved in some kind of church-related work and wait around for heaven!

For these people, the concept of accepting Christ has as its goal a faraway, eternal destination—heaven—rather than the adventure of a present and growing relationship with God. This short-sighted understanding of the Gospel sees being born again as the *goal,* rather than receiving Jesus as the *beginning point* of a totally new life.

When we call on Jesus as Lord and Savior, a new birth takes place; we become as little children. We may have lived fifty years on the planet, but now we are once again a little child, having to learn how to walk all over again. Inviting Christ into our lives is the beginning of a vast renewal.

Renewing the Mind

Renewal is spoken of in the New Testament as the process that should naturally follow the new birth:

...by the washing of regeneration and renewing by the Holy Spirit, whom He poured out upon us richly through Jesus Christ our Savior....

Titus 3:5,6

And do not be conformed to this world, but be transformed by the renewing of your mind, that you may prove what the will of God is, that which is good and acceptable and perfect.

Romans 12:2

The word "renew" in the New Testament is better understood as *renovation*. It is a renovation in which the Holy Spirit, our resident Teacher, tears down all the old belief systems, the foundations upon which our lives were built, and begins to rebuild us. Our new self finds its source and being in the life of the Lord Jesus, Who is divine love, instead of all the significant people in our lives on whom we had depended in the past.

In this renovating process, we are not passive; it is not something that is done to us in which we play no part. We cannot have a man of God impart it to us in a moment of miracle when he lays his hand upon us, although the prayers and blessings of other believers do play a great part. Rather than the instantaneous miracle that occurs when we pass from death to life in the new birth, renovation is the ongoing work of a lifetime in which we actively cooperate with the Holy Spirit in our faith choices.

The Scripture speaks of this work of renewal in Ephesians 4. Having portrayed the way those outside of Christ live, Paul reminds believers that they have met with Christ and He has taught them an entirely different kind of lifestyle:

But you did not learn Christ in this way, if indeed you have heard Him and have been taught in Him, just as truth is in Jesus, that, in

3

reference to your former manner of life, you lay aside the old self, which is being corrupted in accordance with the lusts of deceit, and that you be renewed in the spirit of your mind, and put on the new self, which in the likeness of God has been created in righteousness and holiness of the truth.

Ephesians 4:20-24

We might paraphrase Paul by saying, "Grow up! Stop acting like baby Christians and begin to be who you really are in Christ. Let the work of renewal proceed."

At the very threshold of this work of renewal is the forgiving of all our enemies and the beginning of a lifelong process of forgiving all who hurt us, day by day. Without forgiveness, there is no true living of the Christian life...a life which gets its very existence in our receiving God's forgiveness through the Lord Jesus Christ. We work out the love which we have received every day as we forgive those who ill-treat us. *Whatever else a believer may be, first and foremost he is a forgiver, giving to others what he so lavishly receives from God.*

Putting Away the Deeds of Darkness

The Scripture describes the darkness of lives outside of Christ in terms of unlove and unforgiveness:

...disobedient, deceived, enslaved to various lusts and pleasures, spending our life in malice and envy, hateful, hating one another.

Titus 3:3

But now, living in the light, we have renounced the old paths of darkness. The follower of Jesus is known by the fact that he is a carrier and doer of the love of Jesus. **By this all men will know that you are My disciples, if you have love for one another** (John 13:35).

The first active expression of the unconditional love of God working in us is forgiving others. It is no surprise to find that when the renewal of our lives begins, high on the list of renovations is to cut ourselves off from the positions of unlove and unforgiveness that belonged to our pre-Christian life. Paul calls the believer to a new walk of love:

Let all bitterness and wrath and anger and clamor and slander be put away from you, along with all malice.

Ephesians 4:31

In case we should think that these words have nothing to do with our own lives, let's look briefly at what they mean:

Bitterness is a condition of our spirit. Some wrong has been done to us and we cling to it, determined that the person or persons responsible will pay for what they have done. The word or deed that hurt us may have been done years ago, but we have clung to it, setting our will to the punishment of the one who hurt us.

We see bitterness all around us: In the adult who still clings to the abuse inflicted upon them as a child—in the dark basement of their inner self, they never cease to hate their abuser; in the grown woman with children of her own, who keeps a large space inside with which to hate her father, brothers, and uncles who sexually abused her as a child; in the man, now a father himself, who still hates his father for physically abusing him as a child; in the woman who has been divorced for ten years and still centers her life around her rage at the man who left her for another woman.

We find some perverse joy in licking old wounds. We return to the hurts again and again, reliving them in a movie we play in the theaters of our minds...a movie in which we are the stars. We see ourselves abused, wronged—but oh so right. Every time we play this movie in our imagination, we hear again what each person said or didn't say, what was done, and how it was done. We cling to our memories because, in our darkened minds, we believe that if we forget, the one who hurt us may go free!

The truth is, that person is not being hurt—we are the ones who are in prison to the memory of the events, and we are continually hurting ourselves! Every time we return to the memory of what was done to us, we reopen the wound, we let the blood run a little more, and we make sure that we feel the pain of the original hurt one more time.

Unforgiveness is probably one of the clearest expressions of the insanity of sin. The person we hate knows little or nothing of what is going on, but we are choosing to hurt ourselves again and again and again.

Bitterness can be passed on as an inheritance from father and mother to son and daughter, from generation to generation. Eventually, the possessors of the hate have forgotten why they hate, except that it would be a betrayal of the family not to!

When the dictatorships of Eastern Europe were overthrown, it was only a matter of months before hatreds that had smoldered for generations, hatreds held in check by force, burst into flame. Old hatreds, passed on from the hearts of grandparents and fathers, exploded in the guns of their sons. Time heals nothing...it only fuels the hatred that continues to grow inside of us year after year.

Bitterness arises from the belief that the person who hurt us owes us and must somehow pay us back. We want the books to be even, and that person must hurt as much as they have hurt us. At the very least, we want them to know that they have hurt us, that we want them to come to us begging and groveling, asking for our friendship to be restored.

Ephesians 4:31 indicates that bitterness never stands alone, but it brings a large family along with it: **wrath...anger...clamor...slander...malice....** When any of these are present, it is more than possible that bitterness is buried somewhere down deep inside.

Wrath is violent, explosive rage, whereas **anger** is rage imploded, settling down inside. At times it sneaks out in sarcasm and hurtful actions, but, most of the time, it is expressed in depression.

Clamor is an old expression for uncontrolled temper, shouting and yelling at one another. These outbursts are usually not directed at the person who is the focus of our resentment, but to everyone else in our pathway!

Slander, or gossip, is talking about people behind their backs with a view toward destroying their good reputation and character. This is closely related to evil speaking, which is deliberately saying something that is meant to hurt the hearer; it is also the heart that enjoys and savors hearing evil of another person.

Malice includes all of these expressions; it wants another person to be hurt because of what they have done—in fact, simply because of who they are.

To the person harboring bitterness and any of its unsavory family members, the command of the Spirit is plain, "Put away...." In English, this is not a strong enough phrase to describe the meaning of the words that are used in the original language. It is calling us to a deliberate and immediate choice in which we now cut ourselves off from all such mental and emotional activity.

We could read, "Put it away, do it, and do it now! Don't tell me you'll try—do it! Don't pray about it, but do it now!" It is a violent expression meaning to take it and throw it out of the house, bolt the door, and under no circumstances let it back inside.

Renewing our minds and putting away the deeds of darkness are the first steps we take in the process of "holy renovation."

Chapter Two

DON'T BE A

FOOLISH SERVANT

Jesus continually spoke of forgiveness in terms of releasing a person from something we perceive they owe us. Every Christian knows the prayer that Jesus taught His disciples. It contains these words, **And forgive us our debts, as we also have forgiven our debtors** (Matthew 6:12).

On one occasion, Jesus illustrated this statement with a parable which gives us insight into the nature of unforgiveness and bitterness, teaching us how to forgive our enemies. The story is found in Matthew 18:23-35, where Jesus describes a king who wished to settle all outstanding accounts with his servants, including one who owed him 10,000 talents.

A Debt No One Can Pay

The fact that the servant had a personal interview with the king, and the fact that he had access to so much credit, strongly suggests that he was in a position of responsibility. He may have been in charge of the king's finances and the receiver of all the taxes.

His debt of 10,000 talents was astronomical, and we will never understand the story until we understand just how astronomical it was. To compare 10,000 talents with our modern finances, let us have a quick lesson in the money of that day.

An average worker earned 6 denarii a week, and one talent was equal to 6,000 denarii. This means that if the man worked every week of his life earning an average salary and he saved everything, not spending a penny of his wages, it would take one thousand weeks—approximately twenty years—to earn one talent. Taking into account that no one can save every penny he earns, even if he had the best paying job of his day, 10,000 talents could not be paid back in ten lifetimes!

To show it another way, in the days when Jesus used this illustration, the combined taxes collected from Judea, Idumea, Galilee, Samaria, and Perea were only 800 talents! Jesus is drawing us a picture of a man with a debt that could never be paid in a million years, especially considering the interest that would accrue.

To owe the king 10,000 talents meant the king completely controlled the servant's life! Everything he owned belonged to the king and, should anyone give the servant anything, it immediately became royal property. All monies that came into his hands were, technically, the possession of the king he owed.

For this reason, when the man could not pay, **...his lord commanded him to be sold, along with his wife and children and all that he had, and repayment to be made** (Matthew 18:25).

The servant is a perfect picture of man in his relationship to God, owing a debt he cannot pay. That we are servants of God by right of creation, simply by being alive, is a given fact. We were made by God, by His specifications and blueprint, to be for Him and for His glory. Unlike any other creature, we are made in the image and likeness of the Creator and, in order to fulfill our reason for being, we must freely choose to live by the blueprint.

Sin is incurring a debt with God. We have taken the life that belongs to Him and, rejecting His blueprint, have lived our lives according to our own specifications. We now owe Him our life, but that means death to us—it is a debt we cannot pay and live.

Undeserved Mercy

The servant with the uncollectible debt prostrated himself before the king, saying, **Have patience with me, and I will repay you everything** (Matthew 18:26). The literal Greek has him saying, "Give me time" or "Give me an extension." He dared to say that, given a few months, he could pay all! Jesus is describing a man who had no concept of the debt he had accrued.

The king passed over the statement that bordered on the insane and, instead, spoke in a different mode, that of mercy, compassion, and total pardon of the debt (Matthew 18:27). However, debts do not magically disappear!

The word "forgive" means to send away and release, so the debt had to be sent somewhere. In this case, it was sent to the king himself. For the servant to be forgiven, it personally cost the king 10,000 talents.

But the servant does not appear to understand the magnitude of his debt and, therefore, has no comprehension of the infinity of his forgiveness. While everyone may have been saying, "Wonderful king...fortunate servant...," there is certainly no record of this servant extolling the virtues of his monarch. To him, everything is normal; he is forgiven, so what is the excitement about? He has not considered what he did to have such a debt, nor what it cost the king in order for him to be forgiven.

Unforgiveness Compounds the Problem

In this nonchalant mood, he comes upon a fellow servant of the king who owes him 100 denarii. Based on the economics of the day, we could say that he came on someone who owed him 1/600,000th of his debt—a debt that could easily be paid off in five months by an average worker. Compared with his debt so recently forgiven, 100 denarii was loose change in the pocket!

The servant, forgiven of an uncollectible debt, demands that his fellow servant pay him back the 100 denarii. He follows up his demand by physically choking the man, demanding that he pay the debt at once. The man responds with the identical words the forgiven servant had used before the king— **"Have patience with me and I will repay you."** Only this time, it was a reasonable request!

If you think about it, in actual fact, the debt of the 100 denarii never belonged to the unforgiving servant to begin with; it belonged to the king. When you owe 10,000 talents of gold, every denarius that comes into your hands belongs to your debtor.

Everything that this man earned or that came his way was the king's until the debt was paid. Now that the debt was forgiven, he should have forgiven all his debtors because they were so intrinsically bound up in his debt. At worst, he should have turned the man over to the king as actually owing him the money.

Jesus could not have made it clearer! *God is no longer collecting debts from us, which means we can no longer collect debts from each other.*

The forgiven man does not recognize himself in the cry of his fellow servant and throws him into jail until he pays all. All who hear what happened are appalled. This man should be celebrating his release from an impossible debt by forgiving every person who owed him anything!

The concepts of *binding in jail and releasing from debt* are perfect examples of unforgiveness and forgiveness. What feels like a lead weight in our gut when we do not forgive is actually the groaning of our spirit, as we place our fellow human being in the jailhouse, binding them to their debt to us. To forgive is the reversal of this negative scenario. By releasing them from the prison in which we have placed them, we ourselves are set free.

With the man in jail, the 100 denarii would never be paid! While he was free, there was a good possibility it would get repaid...but never from jail. The hell of not forgiving is that everyone loses; what we perceive as being owed to us will never be repaid.

When we hold a person in jail, they cannot go on living, but are locked up and imprisoned in what they did. And bitterness does just that. We lock the person we refuse to forgive into whatever they did to us.

Watching a high diver in the Olympics the other night, the TV camera froze on the twist of his body as he hurtled into the water. I thought at once of bitterness, which freezes a person into the frame of what they did to us. It may have been ten, twenty, or even forty years ago, but we only see them as frozen in that one act.

Whatever the offender did before that, or after that, does not exist to us. Any repentance or change of character cannot get through to us. As far as we are concerned, they may as well have been dead since they hurt us, for we cannot think of them as they are today, but only as they were in the one act of hurting us.

Chapter Three

IMITATING GOD

In the passage from Ephesians 4, that we considered in the first chapter, we are not only called to be done with bitterness, but to immediately take up new goals and attitudes. We are, in fact, to take up the heart of God and forgive as He has forgiven us. We are to choose to be lovers of others with God's own kind of love.

...forgiving each other, just as God in Christ also has forgiven you. Therefore be imitators of God, as beloved children; and walk in love, just as Christ also loved you....

Ephesians 4:32-5:2

In these few words, the totally supernatural character of living the Christian life is summed up.

We are to love and forgive...just as God has loved and forgiven us!

We Choose to Forgive

We must face the fact that the entire Bible holds us responsible for every thought, imagination, spoken word, and action that we do. The passage we have under consideration says that *we* must put off the bitterness and *we* must forgive. It does not say that it is going to be done for us. Paul does not exhort the believers to let Jesus achieve forgiveness for them; *they* are to forgive even as they have been forgiven.

Believers are crippled by the paralysis of the world which refuses any responsibility for thoughts or actions. The key phrase is "I can't help it," and it is accompanied by an inertia which drifts through life *reacting* to everything and everyone rather than *acting* responsibly.

Thus, when we read such commands as these, that call upon us to put away bitterness and to forgive, they do not register. We want someone else to pray for us and bring about a miracle in us; we want to lie back and let Jesus bring to pass the needed action quite independently of our own will and obedience.

No! He commands us to choose! We are commanded to will the will of God. But that must not be confused with dead legalism, which grits its teeth to try in its own strength to keep God's commands. Legalism will always end in frustration and sin! We are called to will the will of God because God has already worked His miracles in our life.

The first choice we make in agreement with God's will for our lives is the new birth, when we change families. Then, in the middle of the Ephesians passage, we have the key phrase that directs our new life in Christ, **Be imitators of God, as dear children.**

To be a Christian is to actually receive Christ to live in us, communicating His life to us by His Spirit. We do not try to imitate a Jesus in a distant heaven; Jesus, living within us, lives His life through our faith choices.

Because we have been forgiven and have received the love nature of our Father...and our life is now Christ, it is incompatible with our faith to harbor unforgiveness and bitterness. We have been received into His family, and forgiveness of all who have done evil to us is a must.

In Ephesians 4:1, we are called to walk in a manner worthy of the calling with which we have been called. This is an old English way of saying, "Walk in balance," walk through life with your actions in harmony with or balancing out what you believe. Paul is saying, "You have believed in and responded to Love Himself calling you to a lifestyle of love; now let the way you conduct yourselves demonstrate your faith."

Supernatural Empowering

It is not as humans that we try to imitate God, however. That would be impossible and foolish, bringing only condemnation as we continually fail. The Word of God tells us it can be done only because we are God's children, as we partake of His life, which is Christ Himself, who lives in us by His Spirit.

Christ lives within the believer, but what is overlooked by so many is that we need to be supernaturally empowered to translate that life into actions. When Jesus lived on earth, He did so in constant dependence upon the power of the Holy Spirit. *It is the Holy Spirit who gives to us the supernatural power which enables us to put into practice the person we now are, acting in union with Christ Jesus.*

These words we are considering, which command us to act out our faith and forgive, come in chapter 4 of Ephesians, *after* earlier chapters clearly tell of the incredible power that is now residing in us and available to us:

...surpassing greatness of His power toward us who believe...in accordance with the working

of the strength of His might which He brought about in Christ, when He raised Him from the dead, and seated Him at His right hand in the heavenly places, far above all rule and authority and power and dominion, and every name that is named....

Ephesians 1:19-21

In Ephesians 3:14-21 Paul prays that we may be **strengthened with power through His Spirit in the inner man**. He finishes the prayer with a shout of triumph to the God who is **able to do exceeding abundantly beyond all that we ask or think, according to the power that works within us....**

Another example of this power is in Colossians 1:11: **...strengthened with all power, according to His glorious might, for the attaining of all steadfastness and patience...**

The words which are found throughout these prayers, **strengthened** and **power,** are almost the same in the Greek and are defined for us in Acts 1:8. They both speak of the supernatural power imparted to us by the Holy Spirit. The word "strengthen" was used in classical Greek to describe an empowering, enabling someone to act beyond the boundaries of human strength; it was the word to describe the power of a superhero. Today's equivalent would be Superman.

This superhuman power is given to us, not just to raise the dead, but to accomplish steadfastness and patience. **Patience**, in the Greek language, means loving and continuing to love the unlovable. But it means more than that for the believer. It means that whatever that unlovable person does to me, he cannot drag me down to his level and make me hate him or hurt him. *Patience is a word that describes the opposite of getting even.*

A Scripture we are more familiar with is Galatians 5:22: **But the fruit of the Spirit is love....** The love that characterizes a believer is not to be confused with human love. It is not something that we create out of our own human ability, but comes from God Himself, who lives and energizes us from within by His Spirit.

I cannot emphasize this point strongly enough. Although we outline steps which will lead to forgiveness, there is no real forgiving unless we are empowered by the Spirit to love and, therefore, to forgive. As we choose to forgive, we call on the Spirit who lives within us to give us His ability—He actually communicates the life of Jesus to us and through us.

We should not expect a rush of power that can be felt, either. It is usually in looking back that we are amazed that we were able to forgive as we did and to recognize that His power was working in us:

...it is no longer I who live, but Christ lives in me...(Galatians 2:20).

And so, we are responsible as those made in His image with free choice; if we are joined to Christ and empowered by His Spirit, then we can—and must—put away all that is incompatible with Him. We put away bitterness as we would put a disgusting object out of doors.

Understanding Forgiveness

Many believers do not forgive because of misconceptions of what forgiving another person really entails; in most cases, they have an exaggerated view of what takes place. Understanding what we are being called upon to do will help us bring ourselves to obey the command of God. But, first of all, it will help us to understand what forgiving someone is *not*.

Forgiveness is not absolving a person's sin. When a person has deeply wounded us, to forgive them does not mean that we pronounce their sin pardoned. That is between the person and God, to Whom they are responsible for what they did to you.

In other cases, I find people hold back from forgiving their enemy because they feel that in so doing, they are surrendering to him and letting him win. These people look at forgiveness as the act of giving in to evil, of becoming a doormat for the abuser to walk all over. Actually, the reverse is true. When we forgive, for the first time we are really in control!

The person who lives in bitterness is dominated by their enemy; their every thought is darkened and, in some way, controlled by the bitter remembrances of what someone said or did to them. This person mistakenly believes that they have enslaved the one they do not forgive, but the truth is, they have become their offender's lifelong slave.

The offender is never far from the edge of their thoughts, dictating their moods and the way they act in every situation. To forgive means that they are free to get on with life, and their enemy no longer has any power over them.

Many times, believers are caught up in the lie that forgiving means betraying themselves. It is seen as giving a phony smile and brushing the matter aside: "Aw, that was nothing. Everything is just fine! I made a mountain out of a molehill; let bygones be bygones." Any sane person rebels at such a betrayal of his true self.

We cannot forgive until we admit that we have been hurt. For many believers, this sounds almost like a call to sin! But then, most of those same believers are not mentally or emotionally whole either.

Look through the Psalms of David and see how he readily expresses his anger, grief, and disappointment at the way others have treated him. It should be noted that the psalms were prayers or letters to God and, in them, men of God expressed their deepest feelings to Him.

This is not an invitation to vent our anger at the one who hurt us; nor is it sharing the hurt with *others* in a self-pity banquet. It is telling *God* plainly how we feel and how we have been hurt, and releasing our feelings and hurts to Him, presenting ourselves for His healing.

In some cases, more than one psalm deals with the same hurt. With us, it may take a period of time for us to let God into the deepest hurts of our lives in order for us to be truly healed. It is out of this unloading Godward that we are able to forgive and come to wholeness within.

Another foolish phrase that is bandied around the Christian community is that we are to "forgive and forget." As if the new life in Christ is a form of amnesia! *Forgiving means that we can remember the incident as an item of history, but all the poison has been drained out of it, and it is no longer active in our life today.*

We must also distinguish between forgiveness and reconciliation. *We are to forgive all who hurt us, even as they are hurting us, but it does not mean that we must immediately become fast friends.* It is possible that we shall never be close.

To forgive the child molester does not have to be expressed in making him our babysitter! To forgive an emotionally abusive mother does not mean that we now have to allow her into the house every week to continue her verbal destruction.

Jesus Cancelled All Debt

What then is forgiveness? The word simply means to send away, or to release a person. *When we forgive someone, we send them away, releasing them into the hands of God, the only Judge; in doing so, we are choosing to no longer be that person's judge.*

On the cross, Jesus uttered the words, **Father, forgive them; for they do not know what they are doing** (Luke 23:34). The meaning of this is spelled out with great care in Peter's epistle:

> **For you have been called for this purpose, since Christ also suffered for you, leaving you an example for you to follow in His steps, who committed no sin, nor was any deceit found in His mouth; and while being reviled, He did not revile in return; while suffering, He uttered no threats, but kept entrusting Himself to Him who judges righteously....**
>
> **First Peter 2:21-23**

Let's explore the meaning of some of the phrases and words that are used here.

Leaving an example is an expression taken from the schoolroom, where the student would copy over the script of the teacher and, in this way, learn to write. We are told to copy the way Jesus handled the unjust treatment that was hurled at Him.

It is significant that this is the only time the sufferings and death of Jesus on the cross are referred to as an example. In every other case, His death is seen as unique, in that He is dying for the sins of the world. The fact that this is the only time we are told to use His sufferings as the example of how we should act when unjustly treated makes this a very important text.

Follow in His steps is a beautiful expression that can be pictured in the idea of putting our feet in His footsteps in the sand.

Reviled is a word we do not often use in daily speech anymore. It means to insult or humiliate.

Suffer is an abusive kind of suffering. Jesus was abused in every way in His sufferings, both before the cross and on the cross.

Entrusted Himself is the key phrase to this whole passage. It means to deliver over, to commit, or to release into another's care for them to manage or look after.

The tense of the verbs here indicates that for every abusive blow, every cruel insulting word, and every humiliation, there was a specific release of it by Jesus into His Father's care.

Forgiveness is putting our footsteps in His, learning to forgive by doing as He did, which was to place every hurt into the management of the only Just Judge. We should take all the things we have held in bitterness for these many years, and do as He did, committing every hurt to the Father. From now on, minute by minute, every blow that lands upon us shall be placed in His care.

But everything inside us screams out, "What about justice? Someone has got to pay!" We are so wrapped up in our hurt that we look upon ourself, the one who has been sinned against, as the center of the universe.

Let us face a fundamental fact, and one that will help in our understanding of forgiveness: Primarily, I do not sin against you, nor do you sin against me. *All sin is against God.* Sin is the choice to disobey God and set myself in the center of my universe as a god.

We talk glibly in church of sinning against God, but how do we actually achieve it? *We sin against*

God when we violate the rights of and hurt a person who is His creation—when we act unloving toward another human being. It is *His* command we have violated when we lash out against each other. When someone speaks or does evil against us, we are deeply wounded, *but the sin is against God.*

David took the wife of his next-door neighbor and best friend, Uriah, and had a passionate affair with her. In that, he broke covenant with his friend, abused Bathsheba, Uriah's wife, and sent all of Israel into confusion, as he was their spiritual leader. Moreover, we could go on concerning the shockwaves this sent to the pagan nations all around him, those who had submitted to God because of David. Yet, when he prayed his prayer of repentance, he said, **Against Thee, *Thee only,* I have sinned** (Psalm 51:4).

And what has God done with all the sin that we have done against Him? He has taken the debt to Himself in the person of the Lord Jesus and, by the shedding of His blood, canceled it all. He is the compassionate King who has released us by taking the uncollectible debt and paying it Himself.

My sin against God, which was expressed in hurting you, and your sin against God, expressed in hurting me—all have been canceled in the death and resurrection of the Lord Jesus Christ.

"But," someone cries, "what do I do, caught in the middle? I have been violated, wounded by a very bad person! Someone has got to pay!"

Upon hearing these words, I hear Jesus say, "I paid."

Chapter Four

UNLIMITED POWER THROUGH

RELEASING THE DEBT

When I, as a believer, forgive, I am choosing to cancel the debt that God has already canceled. I am taking sides with God, agreeing with Him, and choosing His love in this situation.

Stephen, the first martyr, was being executed by stoning for his faith in Christ. Through a veil of blood, he looked up at his murderers, foremost among them Saul of Tarsus, and prayed, **Lord, lay not this sin to their charge** (Acts 7:60 KJV).

This verse contains an interesting expression. One might liken it to the waitress bringing the check for your meal and laying it on the table. As your friend goes to pick it up, you give the waitress your American Express card and say, "Put it on my charge."

Stephen's last prayer was that the sin of murder, which was against God, although carried out on his body, would be laid to the charge of another. The only other charge it could be laid to was that of the Lord Jesus.

Forgiveness is the death knoll to the self-for-self mentality, which wants to have the dark wisdom and know-how to get even and the power to hurt my enemy, even as I have been hurt. Self prays unconsciously, "Cancel my sins, but let the blood of Christ stop there. Do not cancel theirs. Let them pay for their own!"

Like the unforgiving servant, we can remain blind to what we have been forgiven and turn to choke the life out of our brother who has hurt us. Or, we can make the same decision Stephen made, to cancel the debt we recognize has already been canceled in the death and resurrection of the Lord Jesus. Once we put to death the self-for-self principle, we then experience the resurrection life of God's love. This resurrection life is joy: joy that is health to our spirit, mind, emotions, and every organ of our body.

Replacing Bitterness with Love

I caution you to be aware that, in releasing a person who has hurt you deeply into the hands of the God of love Who has paid for his sins, your first reaction may well be sadness. *It is the sadness of the flesh that recognizes the reality that you have exercised your will in the power of the Spirit and you are not going to get even.*

This person you have held in "jail" waiting for reparation is released from what he owes. The sadness is very real, but it is not originating in your true self in Christ, but from emotions of the flesh that, until now, have had their way in your life.

At this time, you must ask the Holy Spirit to fill the empty spaces of your life, the corrosive holes that bitterness has etched into you. He alone can fill those holes with the healing love of God for you and in you.

You need His love power to renew your mind, so that the mental habits of eagerly expecting and hoping for your enemy to experience hurt will be erased and replaced with the mind of Christ.

The Limitless Power of Forgiveness

Releasing your offender into God's hands and management is not just a matter of religious words. Not only do we release them from our grasp, but something really does take place—your choice really does release the power of God in that person's life. Most believers do not understand the power their choices, expressed in their words, have over God's activity in other people.

If there is no power in the words which express our will, then prayer is a sick joke. But our words do, indeed, have power. Once the person who has been held by the will of our bitterness has been released to God, he will know God's power in his life as never before. I personally believe that Saul of Tarsus, released to God by the words of Stephen, came to Christ aided by that prayer.

If we do not forgive, we are actually making a choice and sending forth a prayer, "Don't forgive, bless, or speak to this person, God. Leave this one in my hands!" We stand in the way of God working in that person's life.

If prayer in the name of Jesus is our working together with Him to limitless ends, then the prayer in our own name, wrapped up in unforgiveness, hinders Him to similar ends. The king in Jesus' story did not step in and force the forgiven servant to release the unfortunate imprisoned man; that was a matter between servants!

I personally commit to God in the name of the Lord Jesus all prayers prayed against me and all words of unforgiveness intended to bind me. I ask that He would take them and deal with them, thus releasing me and my family from the designs of the evil one against us through unforgiving humans.

The Torment of Unforgiveness

If we do not forgive, we place ourselves in a hell on earth. The story of the unforgiving servant gives, in graphic detail, the pathway of the unforgiver. We will pick up the story again where the other servants see what is going on and feel sorry, not only for the servant in jail, but also for the king who has been made to look like a fool. His honor is at stake here, and when they tell him, he brings in the ungrateful servant.

You wicked slave, I forgave you all that debt because you entreated me. Should you not also have had mercy on your fellow slave, even as I had mercy on you?

Matthew 18:32,33

The king calls him *wicked*. The term does not refer to his forgiven debt, for that is over and done with and is no longer under discussion. The wickedness refers to the hardness of his heart, which resulted in his cold refusal to have compassion on his brother in the same way the king had had compassion on him.

The compassionate spirit of the king is compared to the mean and unforgiving spirit of the

37

slave. Paul, in the verses already quoted from Ephesians, is certainly echoing these words: **...forgiving each other, just as God in Christ also has forgiven you...walk in love, just as Christ also loved you...**(Ephesians 4:32-5:2).

The story then takes a twist. The original debt, which could not be paid and which demanded that the man and his family be enslaved, had been forgiven. However, the king now alters the terms of that forgiveness. He hands the man over to the "tormentors."

These tormentors must not be thought of as tormenting the man's body with physical torture in a dungeon; they were the king's bill collectors, who tormented his life by showing up every week to take some of his salary.

The servant is a pardoned man who freely goes about his business earning a living, but the bill collectors are there every week to take something out of his salary **until he should repay all that was owed him** (Matthew 18:34).

Obviously, this was not an effort on the part of the king to get his money back. In the first place, the king was not reneging on his word; and then, the magnitude of that original debt was never handled by putting a lien against a salary, but by slavery and imprisonment.

The bill collectors were there to remind the unforgiving slave that there had been a debt, and the pittance they siphoned off his salary made sure he never forgot it. They were tormentors to his hard and unforgiving heart so that he never enjoyed the pardon he had.

Amazingly, the man still doesn't see it and keeps his fellow servant in jail! He still doesn't get his 100 denarii, but he does get the bill collectors. Jesus said that the Father would do this to the unforgiving (Matthew 18:35).

Making Your Own
Heaven or Hell on Earth

The Father, in creating man, originally programmed him to function by love and by forgiveness...which is love in its releasing mode. Every part of our being, body, soul, and spirit, was built to love and, if we are not loving, we are fighting our own being. We are predestined to love; if we do not, then we are fighting against our destiny.

When we harbor hate, resentment, and unforgiveness, we simply do not function! Our bodies pour out acid into our systems, causing all manner of sickness. Our minds become lethargic and uncreative, while our emotions are swamped with depression and despair. *When we cling to unforgiveness as the foolish servant did, then we remove God's hand of protection from our lives. Automatically, we are exposed to mental, emotional, and physical torment.*

Thousands lie in hospitals, live in depression and hopeless despair, or never have a full day of joy and peace because they have thrown a fellow servant in "jail" and will not let him go until they get the 100 denarii. Their lives are full of tormentors of one kind or another.

The tormentor often has to do with guilt; we are restless, sensing something is intrinsically wrong in our lives, but unable to locate the problem. Many times we open ourselves to sickness because we feel we are such sinners that we deserve it.

We continue trying to be forgiven—not knowing what, exactly, it is that we've done—filling our days with anxiety, depression, self-despising, and shame. We walk down the aisle, trying to get saved again and again, being prayed for over and over. We are wide open to every kind of false guilt.

In our spirit, we know we must have missed the mark, but all our begging and pleading with God does not take our torment away. The fact is, what is wrong is the unforgiveness we hold in our heart, and we cannot receive forgiveness until we call our bitterness "sin" and extend forgiveness to the one who has offended us.

We not only bring hell to ourselves, but we also block off the blessing of God from the Body of Christ. It is very possible for one member of the Body to strangle the flow of life to another member through unforgiveness, and God will not step in to sovereignly stop us. Achan was able to bring the whole camp of Israel to defeat through his disobedience (Joshua 7).

It is no use saying that this is not fair! *This is the way it is.* The flip side is that, as I will forgive John for what he did to me, I bring release in every area, not only to John, but to myself and all those who are affected by me and by John. Taken far enough, this includes the whole Body of Christ.

It is time to **Put away bitterness...and forgive.** In summary, how do we do that?

1. We recognize that whatever the other person or persons may have done to us, we are only responsible for how we have acted. We are not responsible for what they did, but we are responsible for harboring bitterness and withholding forgiveness to them. Our unforgiveness is sin and must be acknowledged as such, and forgiveness is received through the blood of Jesus.

2. We can no longer go along with our feelings; it is our will that directs our actions. We must now

41

choose to forgive those who have hurt us, releasing them to God.

We have found in our seminars that great benefit and relief come when you take time alone to write down the names of the persons who have hurt, abused, or violated you in the distant, and not so distant past, making a note beside each name as to what they have done—what they owe you.

In the intelligent consciousness of knowing what you are doing, declare that they are released and they owe you nothing. Their sin is canceled through the blood of Jesus, and you cancel what He has canceled. At that point, scratch out their name or, if written on separate pieces of paper, tear up the paper and celebrate the cancellation of the debt.

3. When the thoughts of bitterness, anger, and self-pity try to gain access to your mind again, as they will, exercise your authority over them, declaring that the person has been forgiven and you refuse to think on the events of the forgiven past.

In forgiving as you have been forgiven, you will begin to experience the unfolding adventure of walking in dynamic union with the Holy Spirit. You will know the love of God Himself being expressed through you in His supernatural power.

Dispensing God's forgiveness to all who have hurt you is at the threshold of your new life. From this day on, you will know by experience what Jesus meant when He said: **I came that they may have and enjoy life, and have it in abundance—to the full, till it overflows** (John 10:10, Amplified Bible).